OUR
CHRISTIAN WORSHIP

RESOURCES
FOR
ADVENT
AND
CHRISTMASTIDE

FRIEDRICH REST

C.S.S. Publishing Company, Inc.
Lima, Ohio

Copyright © 1985 by
The C.S.S. Publishing Company, Inc.
Lima, Ohio

S86 2T

5868 / ISBN 0-89536-761-0

PRINTED IN U.S.A.

TABLE OF CONTENTS

PREFACE

This book is intended to be a companion to the pastor or chaplain whose responsibility involves leading others in the worship of God during Advent and Christmastide. The quickened heart is at home with warm, emotional, yet intellectually acceptable truths of the historic faith.

Experience gained from editing *Worship Aids for 52 Services* (Westminster Press, 1951), *Worship Services for Church Groups* (Christian Education Press, 1962), and *Our Christian Worship: Resources for Palm Sunday Through Easter* (The C.S.S. Publishing Company, Inc., 1977), and serving with others on the Evangelical and Reformed Committee on Liturgics for two terms and later the Commission on Worship of the United Church of Christ for two terms, while concurrently serving as a church worship leader since ordination in 1937, has led to a variety of ways of magnifying the Lord and exalting his name together.

The format of having a paper bound book to slip into the hymnal or bulletin or Bible may commend itself as a real convenience to a pastor or chaplain, especially if the quality of the selected worship aids is thought to be suitable, and if there are enough options to give variety from year to year. One may adapt or add other selected materials as one senses the deeper, spiritual needs of the people under the guidance of God.

A word of explanation may help explain the purpose of the worship aids offered here.

A pastor or other leader of worship may want to offer a prayer in the presence of the choir before the service begins. The options given may be suggestive. The order in which the worship aids are placed is generally the sequence that is used. The worship aids offered are meant to be a convenience rather than a complete order.

When the congregation is gathered together opening sentences or a call to worship may be said. Again, options are given for the sake of choice or convenience or variety from year to year. An invocation asks God to be present in the service of worship.

Toward the beginning of worship, after acts of adoration or praise, a call to the confession of sins is given, followed by one of the confessions of sins, and an assurance of pardon.

During Advent, a candle lighting ceremony lists introductory sentences, reading of a Scripture lesson as suggested in each form (or one of the lessons from cycle A, B, or C in the regular ecumenical lectionary), the lighting of the candle(s), a prayer, and a hymn. Children and youth may wish to help prepare the Advent candles and wreath and assist in the ceremony of lighting the candles. Other themes than what is here presented may be developed to emphasize the themes of Advent and Christmas.

Traditionally, collects are brief prayers designed to collect our thoughts before the reading of the Scriptures.

The ecumenical lectionary provided three Scripture readings and generally a Psalm as well for each of three years. Since other congregations use this same lectionary, with individual adaptations by different denominations, there may be a value in following the same readings the same year. The C readings will be used in 1985-86, the A in 1986-87, the B in 1987-88, followed by the C and A readings in 1988-89 and 1989-90. The B readings would be resumed in 1990-91 and the C in 1991-92. To figure beyond that year, the arithmetical rule is to divide the last two last two digits of the year which begins the cycle by three. When the two digits are evenly divisible by three, the B lessons are used that year, starting in Advent. 1993 would be divisible by 3 ($93 \div 3 = 31$) so the B lessons will start in Advent of 1993, the C in Advent 1994, etc.

The descriptive titles are meant to indicate briefly part of what each Scripture lesson has in store.

The prayers at the altar are sometimes called the General or Pastoral Prayer, often consisting of brief prayers, each with a suitable introduction or address to God before offering the praise or thanksgiving, or stating a request or intercession. Special intercessions and requests may be added when thought to be needed. In some churches the Sunday following a wedding or a funeral or a special celebration may be a suitable time to lift up the joy, concerns, and thanksgiving of many friends. The leader of worship will seek to be sensitive to the needs of the community and world as he/she determines his/her approach in prayer.

Somewhere in the service a word of welcome may be offered. Indications are that there is no general agreement as to when this should be done, whether just before the offertory, when there is already a break in the service, or earlier in the service so that strangers will feel welcome in the house of God.

The offertory sentence may introduce a biblical base for this act in the life of the Christian steward. The offertory prayer or other suitable words of dedication may be offered after the gifts of the people are brought forward.

The blessing or benediction is pronounced just before the choral response or postlude.

Some of the choicest worship aids may be offered more frequently than the others and the beginning of such repetition is noticeable here.

The brief treasury of additional worship resources is offered because of changing circumstances and occasional demands. The leader will want to add, create, revise, or omit sentences as he/she adapts from this as well as other sections of this small book.

Each prayer to be read aloud can be most effective only if read with meaningful realization.

A. Advent

ADVENT HYMNS

ADVENT HYMNS OF WIDEST USAGE

"Come, O Come, Emmanuel"
"Come, Thou Long Expected Jesus"
"Hail to the Lord's Annointed"
"Let All Mortal Flesh Keep Silence"
"Lift Up Your Heads, Ye Mighty Gates"
"Watchman, Tell Us of the Night"

ADDITIONAL ADVENT HYMNS

"Arise, the Kingdom is at Hand"
"Comfort, Comfort Ye My People"
"Christ is the World's True Light"
"There's a Voice in the Wilderness Crying"
"On Jordan's Bank the Baptist's Cry"
"Hark, A Thrilling Voice"
"Wake, Awake, for Night is Flying"
"Hark, the Glad Sound"
"O'er the Distant Mountains Breaking"
"Sleepers, Wake"
"Rejoice, Rejoice, Believers"
"The King of Glory"
"O How Shall I Receive Thee?"

1. FIRST SUNDAY IN ADVENT

PRAYER FOR THE CHOIR

1. All-gracious God, we thank you for putting music in our hearts and melodies with words of joy on our lips. Guide us that in the spirit of reverence we may exalt your name. Through Jesus Christ our Lord. Amen.

2. O God, our Father in heaven, gather up all good thoughts, sincere feelings, and right intentions, that with all our hearts we may join in the joyful singing of praises for all your deeds of strength and glory. To this end bless our worship. For Jesus' sake. Amen.[12]

OPENING SENTENCES OR CALL TO WORSHIP

1. A Responsive Form (Psalm 95:1-3)

Pastor: O come, let us sing to the Lord;
let us make a joyful noise to the rock of our salvation!

**People: Let us come into his presence with thanksgiving;
let us make a joyful noise to him with songs of praise!**

**All: For the Lord is a great God,
and a great King above all gods.**

2. A Responsive Form (Psalm 95:6-7)

Pastor: O come, let us worship and bow down;
let us kneel before the Lord, our Maker!

**People: For he is our God, and we are the people of his pasture,
and the sheep of his hand.**

INVOCATION

1. Almighty God, in your wise providence you have made all ages to be the highway for the coming of your Son. Prepare our hearts to receive the blessing of his presence, promised to all who sincerely gather in his name. Make yourself known to us on this day in Advent. Open the eyes of our understanding, that we may grow in the grace and knowledge of him who came to bring us life, and that more abundantly. Amen.[1]

2. Almighty God, you are the life of all, the help of those who flee to you, and the hope of those who cry to you, look mercifully upon us! Cleanse our minds and hearts that with a clear conscience

and a calm hope we may confidently worship you. Through Jesus Christ our Lord. Amen.[2]

CALL TO CONFESSION OF SINS

1. Let us humbly confess our sins to Almighty God.

2. Let us draw near with a true heart, and confess our sins to God our Father, asking him in the name of our Lord Jesus Christ to grant us forgiveness.[3]

CONFESSION OF SINS

1. O God, Father of him who became the Savior of the world, we confess that we have grievously sinned against you in many ways — not only by outward transgressions, but also by secret desires and thoughts, which we do not fully understand, but which are all known to you. We do earnestly repent of our selfishness, pride, and waywardness; we are heartily sorry; we seek mercy for all of us; for the sake of your dear son, Jesus Christ, our Lord, forgive our sins, and graciously help our weaknesses. Amen.[4]

2. Almighty and most merciful God our Heavenly Father, we humble ourselves before you, under a deep sense of our unworthiness and guilt. We have grievously sinned against you in thought, in word, and in deed. We have come short of your glory, we have broken your commandments, and turned aside every one of us from the way of life. Yet now, O most merciful Father, hear us when we call upon you with penitent hearts, and for the sake of your Son, Jesus Christ, have mercy upon us. Pardon our sins; take away our guilt; and grant us your peace. Purify us, by the inspiration of your Holy Spirit, from all inward uncleanness, and make us able and willing to serve you in newness of life, to the glory of your holy name. Through Jesus Christ our Lord. Amen.[3]

ASSURANCE OF PARDON

1. Hearken now to the comforting assurance of the grace of God, promised in the Gospel to all who repent and believe: As I live, says the Lord God, I have no pleasure in the death of the wicked, but that the wicked turn from his way and live. God so loved the world that he gave his only Son, that whoever believes in him should not perish but have everlasting life.[3]

To as many of you, therefore, who truly repent of your sins, and believe in the Lord Jesus Christ, with full purpose of new obedience, I announce and declare, by the authority and in the name of Christ, that your sins are forgiven, according to his promise in the Gospel. Through Jesus Christ our Lord. Amen.[3]

2. Upon this humble confession which you have made, as a minister of the Lord Jesus Christ, and by his authority, I declare to you, who do truly repent and heartily believe in Jesus Christ, and are sincerely determined to amend your sinful life, the forgiveness of all your sins in the name of the Father and of the Son and of the Holy Spirit. Amen.[6]

COLLECT

1. O God, who wonderfully created, and yet more wonderfully restored, the dignity of human nature: Grant that we may share the divine life of him who humbled himself to share our humanity, your Son Jesus Christ who lives and reigns with you in the unity of the Holy Spirit, one God, for ever and ever. Amen.[4]

2. Almighty God, give us grace that we may cast away the works of darkness and put upon the armor of light, now and in the time of this mortal life, in which your son Jesus Christ came to visit us in great humility; that in the last day, when he shall come again in his glorious majesty to judge both the quick and the dead, we may rise to the life immortal, through him who lives and reigns with you and the Holy Spirit, now and forever. Amen.[8]

ADVENT CANDLES, FIRST SUNDAY IN ADVENT: HOPE[14]

INTRODUCTORY SENTENCES

Leader: Today is the beginning of Advent — the preparation time for celebrating Christ's birth. We are here because God's promises to our ancestors came true when Jesus was born. God's promise is kept each Sunday when we worship because Christ is in our midst. God will keep the promise to come again in glory.

READING OF SCRIPTURE

Read Isaiah 60:2

LIGHTING OF CANDLE
Leader: We light this candle to proclaim the coming of the light of God into our darkness. With the coming of this light there is hope. Because of Christ we not only have hope but believe that good is stronger than evil. God wants us to work for good in this world.

PRAYER
Leader: God, we thank you that Jesus brought hope into our world. By the good news of the Bible you are still bringing hope to people. Help us to be ready to welcome Jesus Christ so that we may think good thoughts and do good deeds and that we may be a people of hope in our world. Amen.

HYMN

ECUMENICAL SCRIPTURE LESSONS FOR CYCLES A, B, AND C
A. Isaiah 2:1-5 Neither Shall They Learn War Anymore
  Romans 13:11-14 The New Day Calls for a New Life
  Matthew 24:36-44 Of That Day or Hour No One Knows
  Psalm 122 Let Us Go to the House of the Lord
B. Isaiah 63:16-64:4 God Works for Those Who Wait for Him
  1 Corinthians 1:3-9 God is Faithful
  Mark 13:32-37 Take Heed, Watch
  Psalm 80:1-7 Restore Us, O God
C. Jeremiah 33:14-16 A Righteous Branch to Spring Forth
  1 Thessalonians 5:1-6 The Day of the Lord Will Come Like
    a Thief in the Night
  Luke 21:25-36 Signs of the Coming of the Lord
  Psalm 25:1-10 Lead Me in Thy Truth, and Teach Me

PRAYERS AT THE ALTAR
Make us ready
O Lord, you have set before us the great hope that your Kingdom shall come on earth, and have taught us to pray for its coming: Make us ready to thank you for the signs of its dawning, and to pray and work for that perfect day when your will shall be done on earth as it is in heaven.[9]

We praise you

O God: We magnify you, we praise you, we thank you for your bountiful providence, for all the blessings of this present life, and all the hopes of a better life to come. Let the memory of your goodness fill our hearts with joy and thankfulness.[10]

Prayer of humility

Let your beauty be upon us, O Lord, transforming our lives from what we are to that which we ought to be, uniting us in a new love, a new grace of service, and a new happiness of obedience. Make us to know that between you and us there is nothing but our own blindness of heart, since you are so near and we are often so far away. Make us one with all your seekers and finders, that at last we may be one with those who triumph over time and death by your grace.[11]

For the church

O God, Father of all mankind, reveal your mercy to all men, and in your goodness regard those for whom we intercede.[5]

We remember before you your Church throughout the world. Heal its divisions. Endow its ministers, missionaries, and teachers with the Spirit of power, that they may by word and life, and with joy and assurance, set forth the grace of the Lord Jesus; and grant to all its people such zeal for the cause of Christ that their number may be increased daily, and your Kingdom advanced.[5]

For our denomination

As for your whole Church on earth, so also we pray for that branch in which you have joined us in Christ; that we may know him more truly, love him more heartily, and serve him more faithfully.[5]

For others

O Lord: Hear our prayers: For all *who serve* in any charge or office, that by your continued help they may be able to please you in all that you have granted them to do.[5]

For our *homes,* that each may be a shelter from sin and care; and for those who carry the burden thereof, that by reason of your abundant mercies they may still praise you.[5]

For the *children,* that they may remember you in the days of their youth, and grow up in your love and strength.[5]

For the *lonely,* the *sorrowful,* the *sick,* and for all in distress and temptation; that you will be their Comforter and Guide, in weakness their Strength, in weariness their Rest, and in every darkness their Light and their Salvation.[5]

For those who serve

For those who seek to make good use of the time, energy, and talents you have made possible, for those who seek new ways of helping others, and for all who would think ahead in a helpful spirit, that they and we may seek your guidance.[12]

For daily watchfulness and prayer

Eternal God, to whom we are grateful for being permitted to enter upon a new Church year: Grant us the grace to pass the time of our sojourn here in daily watchfulness and prayer, patiently looking for the day of your coming in great power and majesty to judge the world in righteousness. Sanctify us wholly and save us from undue love of the world.[13]

Dedication

Since it is of your mercy, O gracious Father, that another day is added to our lives, we here dedicate both our souls and our bodies to you and to your service in a sober, righteous, and godly life; in which resolution confirm and strengthen us, O merciful God, that, as we grow in age, we may grow in grace and in the knowledge of our Lord and Savior Jesus Christ.[7]

WELCOME TO VISITORS

1. We extend a warm welcome to visitors among us today. May this house of God be your spiritual home where you can find strength and guidance for your daily tasks and duties.[12]

2. We are happy to greet you this morning and extend a cordial welcome to all as we worship and serve together.

OFFERTORY SENTENCES

1. Every one to whom much is given, of him will much be required. (Luke 12:48b)

2. The Son of man came to seek and to save the lost. (Luke 19:10)

OFFERTORY PRAYERS

1. Lord of all power and might, you are the giver of all good things: We thank you for inscribing in our hearts the love of your name and nourishing in us the growth of your goodness as revealed through our Savior. Accept these tokens of our love for all your mercies. Amen.[15]

2. O God, the Fountain of all good; we bring you our gifts, according as you have prospered us. Enable us, with our earthly things to give you the love of our hearts and the service of our lives. Let your favor, which is life, and your steadfast love, which is better than life, be with us now and always; through Jesus Christ our Lord. Amen.[38]

BENEDICTION OR BLESSING

1. The grace of the Lord Jesus Christ and the love of God and the fellowship of the Holy Spirit be with you all. Amen. (2 Corinthians 13:14)

2. The peace of God which passes all understanding, keep your hearts and minds in the knowledge and love of God, and of his Son Jesus Christ our Lord; and the blessing of God Almighty, the Father, the Son, and the Holy Spirit, remain with you always. Amen.[7]

2. SECOND SUNDAY IN ADVENT

PRAYER FOR THE CHOIR

1. O God of peace, you have taught us that in returning and rest we shall be saved, in quietness and confidence shall be our strength: By the might of your Spirit lift us, we pray, to your presence, where we may be still and know that you are God. Through Jesus Christ our Lord. Amen.[3]

2. Open our lips, O Lord, that we may praise you; inspire our hearts that we may love you; and direct our thoughts that we may worship you. In praise and love and consecration teach us to glorify your name. Amen.[26]

OPENING SENTENCES OR CALL TO WORSHIP

1. Behold, the dwelling of God is with men. He will dwell with them, and they shall be his people, and God himself will be with them; he will wipe away every tear from their eyes. (Revelation 21:3-4a)

2. Strengthen the weak hands, and make firm the feeble knees. Say to those who are of a fearful heart, "Be strong, fear not! Behold your God . . . He will come and save you." (Isaiah 35:3-4)

INVOCATION

1. O God, you prepared the minds and hearts of men for the coming of your Son, and your Spirit always works to illumine our darkened lives with the light of his Gospel: Prepare now our minds and hearts that Christ may dwell within us and rule in our thoughts and affections as the King of Love and the Prince of Peace. For his sake. Amen.[17]

2. O almighty God, giver of all grace, you pour out upon all who desire it, the spirit of grace and supplication. Deliver us, when we draw near to you, from coldness of heart and wanderings of mind, that with steadfast thoughts and kindled affections we may worship you in spirit and in truth. Through Jesus Christ our Lord. Amen.[18]

CALL TO CONFESSION OF SINS

1. If we confess our sins, (God) he is faithful and just, and will

forgive our sins and cleanse us from all unrighteousness. Let us confess our sins to almighty God.[16]

2. In joy and contrition we come before God. Let us confess our sins.[16]

CONFESSION OF SINS

1. Almighty and most merciful Father, we have erred, and strayed from your ways like lost sheep. We have followed too much the devices and desires of our own hearts. We have offended against your holy laws. We have left undone those things which we ought to have done; and we have done those things which we ought not to have done. But you, O Lord, have mercy upon us. Spare those, O God, who confess their faults. Restore those who are penitent according to your promises declared to mankind in Christ Jesus our Lord. And grant, O most merciful Father, for his sake, that we may hereafter live a godly, righteous, and sober life. To the glory of your holy Name. Amen.[3]

2. Most holy and merciful Father: We acknowledge and confess before you our sinful nature, prone to evil and slothful in good, and all our shortcomings and offenses. You alone know how often we have sinned, in wandering from your ways, in wasting your gifts, in forgetting your love. But, you, O Lord, have mercy upon us, who are ashamed and sorry for all areas in which we have displeased you. Teach us to hate our errors, cleanse us from our secret faults, and forgive our sins, for the sake of your dear Son. And, O most holy and loving Father, help us, we beseech you, to live in your light and walk in your ways, according to the commandments of Jesus Christ our Lord. Amen.[40]

ASSURANCES OF PARDON

1. Beloved, God has promised us his mercy and has given us his Son, Jesus Christ, to die for our sins that we may live in newness of life, obedient to his will. Therefore, I announce in the name of Christ, that your sins are forgiven according to his promises in the Gospel. Amen.[16]

2. God showed his love for us in that while we were yet sinners Christ died for us.

God so loved the world that he gave his only Son, that whoever believes in him should not perish but have eternal life.

There is therefore now no condemnation for those who are in

Christ Jesus. Amen.[16]

COLLECT

1. O God, in whom there is no darkness and whose Son is the light of the world, dispel the darkness of our ignorance and unbelief by the light and love of your Gospel; through Jesus Christ our Lord. Amen.[34]

2. Blessed Lord, you have caused all holy Scriptures to be written for our learning: Grant that we may in such wise hear them, read, mark, learn, and inwardly digest them, that by patience and comfort of your holy Word we may embrace, and ever hold fast, the blessed hope of everlasting life, which you have given us in our Savior Jesus Christ. Amen.[7]

ADVENT CANDLES, SECOND SUNDAY IN ADVENT: PEACE[14]

INTRODUCTORY SENTENCES
Leader: We gather around the Advent wreath today knowing that we are not perfect — that we all make mistakes and do bad things. Only Jesus obeyed God fully. Jesus helps us to live as God wants us to live and Jesus gives us peace.

READING OF THE SCRIPTURE
Read Isaiah 9:6-7

LIGHTING OF CANDLES
Leader: We light this candle to proclaim the coming of the light of God into our darkness. With the coming of this light there is peace, for Christ is called the "Prince of Peace." Christ's name is also Emmanuel, "God is with us." The presence of Christ with us gives us peace day by day.

PRAYER
Leader: Eternal God, we thank you that through all the years you have given peace to your people. Help us to have your peace in our lives. We pray that, in this Advent season, we may, by what we do, show your presence to the sick, the hungry, and the lonely, so that they too may have

peace. Amen.

HYMN

ECUMENICAL SCRIPTURE LESSONS FOR CYCLES A, B, AND C
A. Isaiah 11:1-11 A Branch From the Roots
   Romans 14:4-9
   The Patient Endurance of Hope
   Matthew 3:1-12 John the Baptizer Preaching
   Psalm 72:1-19 Blessed Be the Lord, the God of Israel
B. Isaiah 40:1-5, 9-11 Comfort, Comfort My People
   2 Peter 3:8-14 The Eyes of the Lord are On the Righteous
   Mark 1:1-8 John the Baptizer Baptized with Water
   Psalm 85 Restore Us Again, O God
C. Isaiah 9:2, 6-7 For Unto Us a Child is Born
   Philippians 1:3-11 That Your Love May Abound More and
   More
   Luke 3:1-6 Prepare the Way of the Lord
   Psalm 126 The Lord Has Done Great Things for Us

PRAYERS AT THE ALTAR
Thanks for John the Baptizer and others
O God, we thank you for John the Baptizer and all prophetic spirits who have envisioned the promise of a better day. We thank you for stout-hearted men and women who in days of discouragement have still believed in your goodness and in your desire to lead your people from darkness into light. We rejoice because people of faith in dim centuries dared believe in the coming of One who should bear burdens and redeem people from their sins. For their vision of a Redeemer, and for your response to their desires, we thank you, and pray for a strong faith in our day.[23]

We confess our broken vows
God of truth and love, we acknowledge before you our deep need of a new birth of Christ's spirit in our midst. We confess our own share in the selfishness which rules our human life, in the prejudices and suspicions which divide men, in the love of unworthy things which cheapens life, in the timidity which holds back good causes, and in the indifference which permits evil to go unchecked. We confess our broken vows of loyalty to Christ, our obedience to the powers of evil which he hates, our want of faith in

the way of love.[23]

Thanks for the world above and below

Most gracious God: We thank you for the world you have prepared for our dwelling place, for friends and relatives, for that home of larger seen and unseen followers of your Son, and even the disappointments which remind us that we have here no abiding city.[22]

Bless the world

O God, for whose Spirit our world hungers and thirsts: Bless us with peace and righteousness the world over as the season of good will comes upon us. Let your Spirit rule among the nations, that concord and mutual service may be established, and the mind of Christ bind people with people and race with race in brotherhood.[23]

For the happiness of others

Support all those at this season who think and plan to give happiness to others, and give them the deepest joy in their tasks. Sustain all those who must bear added burdens to provide cheer for others. Help us all to be mindful and considerate of them. Abundantly bless those in whose hearts there is little room for joy because sorrow has come to them. We think of the families of: (include here names of specific families). Grant that in the knowledge of Christ's comfort they may find the peace that knows no end.[23]

Make us fit for service

Draw us nearer to yourself and make us fit for your service. Pour your spirit into our hearts to prompt the most ardent devotion to your service, that we may render our whole life one continued chain of thanksgiving. Guide us toward paths of usefulness and lead us in your way. By the quickening of your Spirit lift our thoughts toward things true, lovely, and of good report, and grant us visions of your kingdom of good will upon earth.[23]

Prepare us for your coming

O Lord and Savior, you are the judge of the living and the dead: Give us grace to cast off the works of darkness and grant us the guidance of your Holy Spirit that we may live in daily preparation of your coming. Purify us, that in your eternal and glorious kingdom, we may become like you. Aid us, O Lord, that at your second coming to judge the world we may be with those on your right hand who behold with joy and uplifted hands the fullness of redemption drawing near; and be pleased to say graciously to us, "Come, O blessed of my Father, inherit the Kingdom prepared for you from the foundation of the world."[24]

WELCOME TO VISITORS

1. Our church extends a cordial welcome to all in the name of the Lord Jesus — the Head of the Church. We hope you will receive a blessing and we invite you to be with us again.

2. You are never a stranger in your Father's house. This is a house of prayer and we invite you to worship with us as often as you can.[12]

OFFERTORY SENTENCE

1. For what does it profit a man, to gain the whole world and forfeit his life? (Mark 8:36)

2. Therefore do not be anxious, saying, "What shall we eat?" or "What shall we drink?" or "What shall we wear?" For the Gentiles seek all these things; and your heavenly Father knows that you need them all. But seek first his kingdom and his righteousness, and all these things shall be yours as well. (Matthew 6:31-33)

OFFERTORY PRAYER

1. We thank you, O heavenly Father, for the privilege of giving to you of that which you have given to us. Help us to understand how to give, as becomes those who receive so richly from your bounty. May this offering be wisely spent and carry a blessing with it. We ask it for your glory. Amen.[6]

2. Most gracious God, you have made us stewards of your bounty, and trusted us with the use of your gifts. We lift up our hearts in thanksgiving for the many evidences of your surrounding love. For all that you are to us, and all that we may be to you, we give thanks to you, not only with our gifts today, but with our lives throughout the week. Through Jesus Christ our Lord. Amen.[23]

BLESSING OR BENEDICTION

1. The Lord bless you, and keep you: The Lord make his face to shine upon you, and be gracious unto you: The Lord lift up his countenance upon you, and give you peace. (Numbers 6:24-26).

2. The grace of the Lord Jesus Christ and the love of God and the fellowship of the Holy Spirit be with you all. Amen. (2 Corinthians 13:14)

3. THIRD SUNDAY IN ADVENT

PRAYER FOR THE CHOIR
1. We come before your presence, O Lord, with thanksgiving and enter your courts with praise. Grant that we may perfectly magnify your name. Through Jesus Christ our Lord. Amen.[26]

2. Grant us, we beseech you, O merciful God, prudently to study, rightly to understand, and perfectly to fulfill that which is pleasing to you, to the praise and glory of your name.

You, O Christ, are the King of glory; you are the everlasting Son of the Father. Amen.[27]

OPENING SENTENCES OR CALL TO WORSHIP
1. A Responsive Form (Isaiah 40:3-6)

Pastor: In the wilderness prepare the way of the Lord, make straight in the desert a highway for our God.

People: Every valley shall be lifted up, and every mountain and hill be made low; the uneven ground shall become level, and the rough places a plain.

Pastor: And the glory of the Lord shall be revealed, and all flesh shall see it together.

People: For the mouth of the Lord has spoken.

2. A Responsive Form (Isaiah 35:3-7a)

Pastor: Strengthen the weak hands, and make firm the feeble knees. Say to those who are of a fearful heart, "Be strong, fear not! Behold, your God will come with vengeance, with the recompense of God. He will come and save you!"

People: Then the eyes of the blind shall be opened, and the ears of the deaf unstopped; then shall the lame man leap like a hart, and the tongue of the dumb sing for joy. For waters shall break forth in the wilderness, and streams in the desert; the burning sand shall become a pool, and the thirsty ground springs of water.

INVOCATION
Eternal Father: As we worship in your house, prepare us to rejoice as the shepherds rejoiced at the sound of the angels' song.

Fill us with joy as we hear again the story of your love. As the Wise Men brought their gifts to the Christ-child, help us to bring the richest treasures of our devotion and lay them before your majesty. As seekers in the past followed tha star that led them to the shrine of his birth, prepare our hearts for the fulfillment of our need, that in this hour of worship we may find you, and be led to life eternal. Through Jesus Christ our Lord. Amen.[1]

2. O God, you have promised to be an everlasting light to your people, we thank you most heartily for his coming. Mercifully grant that all hearts may be filled with the spirit of good will, that peace and righteousness and friendliness may cover the earth. In the name of Jesus Christ, the Prince of Peace. Amen.

CALL TO CONFESSION

1. Since the Lord is gracious and full of compassion, slow to anger, and of great mercy, we come confidently to the throne of grace and ask God to forgive us. Let us confess our sins together.[12]

2. If we say that we have no sin, we deceive ourselves, and the truth is not in us. But if we confess our sins, he is faithful and just to forgive us our sins, and to cleanse us from all unrighteousness.[6]

Let us therefore confess our sins to God, and humbly beseech him, in the name of our Lord Jesus Christ, to grant us forgiveness, saying:[6]

CONFESSION OF SINS

1. Almighty and most merciful God our heavenly Father, we humble ourselves before you, under a deep sense of our unworthiness and guilt. We have grievously sinned against you, in thought, in word, and in deed. We have come short of your glory, we have broken your commandments, and turned aside every one of us from the way of life. Yet now, O most merciful Father, hear us when we call upon you with penitent hearts, and for the sake of your Son, Jesus Christ, have mercy upon us. Pardon our sins; take away our guilt; and grant us your peace. Purify us, by the inspiration of your Holy Spirit, from all inward uncleanness, and make us able and willing to serve you in newness of life, to the glory of your holy Name; through Jesus Christ our Lord. Amen.[56]

2. Almighty and most merciful Father, we have erred, and strayed from your ways like lost sheep. We have followed too much

the devices and desires of our own hearts. We have offended against your holy laws. We have left undone those things which we ought to have done; and we have done those things which we ought not to have done. But you, O Lord, have mercy upon us. Spare those, O God, who confess their sins. Restore those who are penitent, according to your promises declared to mankind in Christ Jesus our Lord. And grant, O most merciful Father, for his sake that we may hereafter live a godly, righteous, and sober life, to the glory of your holy name. Amen.[56]

ASSURANCE OF PARDON

1. Hear the promises of God: Ask, and it will be given you; seek, and you will find; knock, and it will be opened to you. If we confess our sins, he is faithful and just, and will forgive our sins.

I announce therefore in the name of Jesus Christ that your sins are forgiven. Amen.[16]

2. The kingdom of heaven is at hand. The Lord is with us. May you be blessed with an assurance as deep as that of the Apostle Paul, who said, "Neither death, nor life, nor angels, nor principalities, nor things present, nor things to come, nor powers, nor height, nor depth, nor anything else in all creation, will be able to separate us from the love of God in Christ Jesus our Lord." Amen.[12]

COLLECT

1. Almighty God, our Father, we remember that you have declared your holy will through prophets and apostles, raising up a ministry for your holy Word, and we pray you to inspire the lips of all who declare your Gospel, and to illumine by your Holy Spirit the minds of all who hear, through Jesus Christ our Lord. Amen.[35]

2. O God, as you challenged Israel through the stern words of John the Baptizer, arouse us who are at ease and sleeping in our sins, that we may hear the criticism and comfort of the Gospel and prepare a highway in our hearts for the coming of Jesus Christ, our Lord. Amen.[34]

ADVENT CANDLES, THIRD SUNDAY IN ADVENT: LOVE [14]

INTRODUCTORY SENTENCES

Leader: As we gather around the Advent wreath today, we rejoice that Christmas is a time of prayer and of open
hearts when we sing songs of joy. Christmas is a time
of worship- the moment when the busiest of us pause
in wonder. Christmas happens when God comes to us
in love through Jesus Christ and fills us with love for
all humankind.

READING OF SCRIPTURE
Read 1 John 4:9-11

LIGHTING OF CANDLES
Leader: We light this candle to proclaim the coming of the
light of God into our darkness. With the coming of
this light there is love. Such great love helps us to
love both God and one another.

PRAYER
Leader: O God, we thank you that Jesus showed your love
for every person — babies and children, old people
and young, sick people and those who were strong,
rich people and those who were poor. Come to us in
this Advent season, and give us love in our hearts for
all persons. Amen.

HYMN

ECUMENICAL SCRIPTURE LESSONS FOR CYCLE A, B, AND C
A. Isaiah 35:1-6, 10 Be Strong, Fear Not
James 5:7-10 Patient Waiting for the Lord
Matthew 11:2-11 John's Message to Jesus
Psalm 146 Put Not Your Trust in Princes
B. Isaiah 61:1-4, 8-11 The Office of Christ
1 Thessalonians 5:16-24 Hold Fast What is Good
John 1:6-8, 19-28 The Testimony of John
Luke 1:46b-55 The Magnificat of Mary
C. Zephaniah 3:14-18 The Lord Your God is in Your Midst
Philippians 4:4-9 Rejoice in the Lord Always
Luke 3:10-18 One Mightier Than I is Coming
Isaiah 12:2-6 God is My Salvation

PRAYERS AT THE ALTAR
Blot out our transgressions

Have mercy upon us, O God, according to your loving kindness; according to the multitude of your tender mercies blot out our transgressions. Wash us thoroughly from our iniquities and cleanse us from our sins. For we acknowledge our transgressions and our sins are ever before us. Purge us, and we shall be clean; wash us, and we shall be whiter than snow. Create in us clean hearts, O God, and renew a right spirit within us. Cast us not away from your presence, and take not your holy Spirit from us. (Psalm 51)

HELP US TO MAKE ROOM

Merciful God, our heavenly Father: We praise you for the blessings of this sacred season. Grant us grace and heavenly wisdom that we may receive your Word with pure affection and bring forth the fruits of your Spirit.[6]

Eternal Christ: As we approach another Christmas when the world remembers your birth, cause us who bear your name to make room in the inner chambers of our hearts. Create in us an understanding of the deep significance of your coming and make us responsive to all that it means to the world.[1]

Come, Lord Jesus, our blessed Savior, and manifest your presence among us; revive your languishing people. Bestow upon us the help of your Holy Spirit, that we may daily increase in your knowledge; confess, honor, and worship you; take up our cross and follow you; and always walk as the children of light.[37]

INTERCESSIONS FOR INDIVIDUALS

O God of mercy, you hear our prayers for others: We plead for those who are lonely. Through new associations and activities and observations, give them consolations as may be needful.

We entreat you on behalf of those who feel discouraged or disappointed; restore courage, hope, and conviction to them, whereby they may have newness of life.

We ask that you comfort those who are ill. By the knowledge that all things work together for the good to those who love you, enable them to await your healing with patience; your peace with hope; your house of many rooms with faith.

We entreat you to give strength and power to all who are seriously working for the welfare of their community and country; but

4. FOURTH SUNDAY IN ADVENT

PRAYER FOR THE CHOIR
1. O God of all goodness: help us to praise you for the wonderful gift of your Son. Give us such happiness within that we may lead others in joyful worship. Amen.[12]

2. As we worship here today, we ask you, Father, to put a new joy in our hearts, a new confidence in our wills, a new truth in our minds, a new task in our hands, and a new song in our mouths. Amen.[33]

OPENING SENTENCES OR CALL TO WORSHIP
1. In the Form of a Response (Psalm 130:5-7)

Pastor: I wait for the Lord, my soul waits, and in his Word I hope;

People: My soul waits for the Lord more than watchmen for the morning . . .

Pastor: O Israel, hope in the Lord!

People: For with the Lord there is steadfast love, and with him is plenteous redemption.

2. In the Form of a Response (Isaiah 55:6-7)

Pastor: Seek the Lord while he may be found,

People: Call upon him while he is near;

Pastor: Let the wicked forsake his way, And the unrighteous man his thoughts;

People: Let him return to the Lord, that he may have mercy on him, and to our God, for he will abundantly pardon.

INVOCATION
1. Almighty and ever blessed God: We thank you that we are permitted once again to rejoice with your holy Church in the season of Advent. Grant that this approach to Christmas (Day) may be hallowed by devout meditation. Keep the thought of your love bright in our hearts, that we may be joyful. Empower us with childlike expectations and simple faith to look for the coming of your Son into our hearts, that we may in this hour worship you, and in the time that follows spread peace and good will to people. Through Jesus Christ our Lord. Amen.[36]

2. We thank you, O Father, for preparing a road through your wilderness, for revealing the way to us through your Son; for supplying all our needs, but above all, the needs of our soul; for initiating a discussion with us; and for challenging us to seek ever expanding frontiers. So often we experience dryness of spirit, joylessness of heart, and weakness of will. We come to you therefore, because you have come to us with the gift of life. We rejoice in your goodness, and praise you for the hope given to us through the incarnation, crucifixion, and resurrection of your Son, Jesus Christ our Lord. Amen.[25]

CALL TO CONFESSION OF SINS

1. If we claim to be sinless, we are self-deceived and strangers to the truth. If we confess our sins, God is just, and may be trusted to forgive our sins and cleanse us from every kind of wrong.[67]

Let us admit our sin before God:[67]

as our Savior, Redeemer, and Lord, we dare come with confidence as we approach him in prayer. Let us now ask God to forgive us.[12]

CONFESSION OF SINS

1. Gracious God, Father of our Lord Jesus Christ, you have promised to receive us when we come to you. We confess that we have sinned against you in thought, word, and deed. We have disobeyed your law. We have not loved you or our neighbors as we should. Forgive us, O God, and grant that we may live and serve you in newness of life through Christ our Lord. Amen.[16]

2. Gracious God, Creator and Father, we come before you as a rebellious people. We have denied your intentions for us; we have preferred our way to Christ's way; we have disobeyed your commandments; and we have worshiped ourselves and the things we have made. Forgive us, restore in us the knowledge of who we are, and make us alive to serve you in faith, obedience, and joy; through Jesus Christ our Lord. Amen.[16]

ASSURANCE OF PARDON

1. Beloved, God has promised us mercy and has given us his Son, Jesus Christ, to die for our sins that we may live in newness of life, obedient to his will. Therefore, I announce, in the name of Christ, that your sins are forgiven according to his promises in

the Gospel. Amen.[16]

2. God shows his love for us in that while we were yet sinners Christ died for us.

God so loved the world that he gave his only Son, that whoever believes in him should not perish but have eternal life.

There is therefore now no condemnation for those who are in Christ Jesus. Amen.[16]

COLLECT FOR THE FOURTH SUNDAY IN ADVENT

1. Blessed Lord, through whose gift of the holy Scriptures we learn of your mighty saving acts for humankind, help us so to hear, remember, and understand your holy Word that, strengthened and sustained thereby, we may know in this temporal life the hope of eternity which you have given us in our Savior Jesus Christ, who lives and rules with you and the Holy Spirit, now and ever. Amen.[45]

2. Jesus, begotten of the Father, born of Mary; make this holy season a reminder to us that as you once entered the realm of time and space so still you enter our earthly existence with your divine presence. Make this knowledge the source of our Christmas joy, the cause of our hymns of praise, and the occasion of our prayers of thanksgiving. Amen.[46]

ADVENT CANDLES, FOURTH SUNDAY IN ADVENT: JOY

INTRODUCTORY SENTENCES

Leader: Soon we shall celebrate the birth of Jesus. We worship God with joy in our hearts as we are reminded of the words the angel said on that first Christmas Day, "Behold, I bring you good news of a great joy which will come to all the people." (Luke 2:10)

READING OF SCRIPTURE

Read John 15:9-11

LIGHTING OF CANDLES

Leader: We light this candle to proclaim the coming of the light of God into our darkness. With the coming of

this light there is joy joy that is ours not only at
Christmas but always.

PRAYER

Leader: O Holy One, as Christmas draws near, there is a
sense of excitement in the air. We can feel a joy in
our lives and see it in those around us. Still, for
some of us this is a sad time because of unhappy
things that have happened in our lives. Help us to
have the joy that does not depend upon earthly happiness but upon you. Help us to be filled with your
joy so that we may share it with a joyless world.
Amen.

HYMN

ECUMENICAL SCRIPTURE LESSONS FOR CYCLES A, B, AND C

A. Isaiah 7:10-15 A Young Woman Shall Conceive and Bear
a Son
Romans 1:1-7 Grace to You and Peace from God
Matthew 1:18-25 The Birth of Jesus Took Place in This Way
Psalm 24 Lift Up Your Heads, O Gates
B. 2 Samuel 7:8-16 I Have Been With You Wherever You Went
Romans 16:25-27 To The Only Wise God Be Glory
Luke 1:26-38 The Annunciation to Mary
Psalm 89:1-4 Blessed Are the People Who Know
C. Micah 5:1-4 From You Shall Come Forth a Ruler
Hebrews 10:5-10 The Offering of the Body of Jesus Christ
Psalm 80:1-7 Restore Us, O God

PRAYERS AT THE ALTAR
Thanks for John the Baptizer

Almighty God, who by the mouth of your holy prophets
proclaimed the coming of the Redeemer of the whole world: We
praise you that you sent John the Baptizer to prepare the way for
your Son Jesus Christ. Grant, O God, that the voice of your servant in the wilderness may move the hearts of all people to prepare a highway for the Savior of the world, that the good tidings
of great joy may be brought to all, and every tongue confess that
Jesus Christ is Lord, to your praise and glory.[37, 6]

Prayer for Confession

Almighty God, our Heavenly Father, you caused the light to shine out of darkness in the advent of our Lord Jesus Christ to take away the sins of the world: We humbly confess our transgressions and implore your forgiveness. We are ashamed of that within us which makes neither for good will to others nor for growth in goodness in our own lives. We beseech you that the Spirit of Christ may be born anew within us, and that we may glorify his nativity, with hearts of compassion, deeds of kindly service, and the spirit of good will to all humankind.[64]

For our Christmas plans

We commit to you, O God, in this silent hour, all our Christmas plans, our hopes, our daily work, our families and family reunions, our gaieties and our griefs — asking your blessing upon every thought and endeavor, your control over every enterprise, your spirit of love in our hearts and wisdom in our minds.[41]

Be with our waiting earth

God of love, in whose providence your world once echoed with the heavenly songs of "Peace on earth, good will to men;" shed abroad throughout the earth your Spirit until ancient animosities be forgotten and lingering prejudices disappear, and no want goes unrelieved, and all humankind bows before the Prince of Peace. Visit in your sympathy all who from the shadows of loneliness and sorrow look upon joy in which they find no share, and grant to them the Christmas peace which passes knowledge. Grant the power of his Spirit to all who beneath the guide of mirth do battle with temptations which daily press them hard, and make them more than conquerors through him who strengthens.[23]

For the healing ministry

Lord Jesus, who in the days of your earthly life went about healing people from all manner of sickness and disease: Be with those who work in our hospitals to rescue our brothers and sisters from illness of the body, and give us all such a measure of your spirit that our comings and goings among our neighbors may bring soundness of body, mind, and spirit. This we desire in thankfulness to you.[39]

For divine support

O Lord, support us all the day long of this troublous life, until the shadows lengthen and the evening comes, and the busy world is hushed, and the fever of life is over, and our work is done. Then in your great mercy grant us a safe lodging, and a holy rest, and peace at the last. Through Jesus Christ our Lord. Amen.[65]

WELCOME TO VISITORS

1. We open wide the doors of this church to all who desire sincerely to worship the heavenly Father, whom Jesus so clearly revealed. We offer the services of our church for the renewal of the spiritual life, the encouragement of the languishing heart, the consecration of the strong, and for the ever deepening assurance of life eternal.

2. In whatever household of faith into which you were born, whatever creed you now profess, whatever your nationality or ethnic origin, you have come to this sanctuary where you are welcome, since this is a house of prayer for all people.

OFFERTORY SENTENCE

1. He must reign until he has put all his enemies under his feet. (1 Corinthians 15:25)

2. Freely ye have received, freely give. (Matthew 10:8 K.J.)

OFFERTORY PRAYER

O great Giver of all good and perfect gifts, you have given us your Son, Jesus Christ as a Babe in Bethlehem for our enlightenment and salvation. Accept these gifts of our love for you and your Son, and grant that the light which shone 'round about the hills of Bethlehem may give us a Christmas peace passing all understanding; through Jesus Christ our Lord. Amen.[12]

2. Almighty God, we pray that these offerings may be used for the glory of your name, in the proclamation of the Gospel, the confirmation of your Church, and the coming of your Kingdom. Through Jesus Christ our Lord. Amen.[29]

BLESSING OR BENEDICTION

1. The grace of the Lord Jesus Christ and the love of God and the fellowship of the Holy Spirit be with you all. (2 Corinthians 13:14)

2. The Lord bless you, and keep you: The Lord make his face shine upon you, and be gracious unto you: The Lord lift up his countenance upon you, and give you peace. Amen. (Numbers 6:24-26)

B. Christmastide

CHRISTMAS CAROLS OF WIDEST USAGE
"O Come, All Ye Faithful"
"Silent Night! Holy Night!"
"Joy to the World!"
"Hark, the Herald Angels Sing"
"Angels, From the Realms of Glory"
"While Shepherds Watched Their Flocks by Night"
"It Came Upon the Midnight Clear"
"O Little Town of Bethlehem"
"Away In a Manger"
"Christians, Awake, Salute the Happy Morn"
"Good Christian Men, Rejoice"
"All My Heart This Night Rejoices"
"As With Gladness Men of Old"
"Once in Royal David's City"
"The First Noel"

ADDITIONAL CHRISTMAS CAROLS
"Angels We Have Heard on High"
"A Stable Lamp is Lighted"
"Calm on the Listening Ear of Night"
"Hark, the Angel Voices Singing"
"Come All Ye Shepherds, Ye Children of Earth"
"Break Forth, O Beauteous Heavenly Light"
"Behold, A Branch is Growing"
"Every Star Shall Sing"
"From Heaven Above to Earth I Come"
"O Thou Joyful, O Thou Wonderful"
"My Master Was So Very Poor"
"On Christmas Night"
"On a Day When Men Were Counted"
"Go Tell It on the Mountain"
"On This Day Earth Shall Ring"
"O Thou Who By a Star Didst Guide"
"Every Star Shall Sing a Carol"
"Come Hither, Ye Children"

5. CHRISTMAS

PRAYER FOR THE CHOIR
1. O Father, you have declared your love to the world by the birth of the Holy Child of Bethlehem: Help us as we enter the sanctuary, to serve sincerely, with a purity of heart, that all may worship with gladness and make room for him in their hearts. In his name. Amen.[4]

2. O Lord God, you have taught us to pray together, and have promised to hear the united voices of even two or three invoking your name; hear now, O Lord, the prayers of our servants and give us, in this world, knowledge of your truth and, in the world to come, life everlasting; for the sake of Jesus Christ our Lord. Amen.[47]

OPENING SENTENCES OR CALL TO WORSHIP
1. In A Responsive Form (Isaiah 9:6)
Pastor: For to us a child is born, to us a son is given;
People: And the government will be upon his shoulder, and his name will be called
All: "Wonderful Counselor, Mighty God, Everlasting Father, Prince of Peace."

2. Sing for joy, O heavens, and exult, O earth; break forth, O mountains, into singing! For the Lord has comforted his people. (Isaiah 49:13)

INVOCATION
1. O God, who centuries ago blessed our earth with a vision of your love in the form of a little Child: Once more gladden us with the light that shone around the hills of Bethlehem. Graciously grant us a true Christmas blessing as we worship. Fill our hearts with gratitude. And lead us into the Christmas peace which passes all understanding, the peace of your Son and our Lord. Amen.[23]

2. O Lord, you are the way, the truth, and the light; in whom there is no darkness, error, vanity, or death — the light without which there is darkness; the way without which there is wandering; the truth without which there is error; the life without which there is death. Let there be light, and we shall see light and we shall shun darkness; we shall see life and escape death: Illuminate

our blind souls which sit in darkness and the shadow of death; and direct our feet into the way of peace. Amen.[48]

3. Almighty God, to you all hearts are open, all desires known, from you no secrets are hidden: Cleanse and inform the thoughts of our hearts by the inspiration of your Holy Spirit, that we may truly love you and worthily praise your holy name, through Jesus Christ our Lord. Amen.[58]

CALL TO CONFESSION OF SINS

1. If we confess our sins, God is faithful and just, and will forgive our sins and cleanse us from all unrighteousness. Let us confess our sins to almighty God.[16]

2. Let us draw near with a true heart, and confess our sins to God our Father, asking him in the name of our Lord Jesus Christ, to grant us forgiveness.[16]

CONFESSION OF SINS

1. Our heavenly Father, by your love you have made us, and through your love have kept us, and in your love would make us perfect; we humbly confess that we have not loved you with all our heart and soul and mind and strength, and we have not loved one another as Christ has loved us. Forgive us for what we have been; help us to amend what we are; and with your Holy Spirit direct what we shall become; through Jesus Christ our Lord. Amen.[49]

2. O God, you have given us light and you grieve because we have so often loved the darkness better; you have called us to follow that which is good, and to flee from that which is evil; yet you know we have yielded to the temptations in our path, have done that which is forbidden, and have left undone the work you have given us to do. O God, we have paid so little attention to your voice of warning and guidance. Call us yet again, that we may answer and do your bidding, that we may not go astray from you any more; but, being comforted by your love, and upheld by your strength, we may fulfill our days upon earth, forgiven and at peace with you. Amen.[50]

ASSURANCE OF PARDON

1. Beloved, God has promised us his mercy and has given us his Son, Jesus Christ, to die for our sins that we may live in

newness of life, obedient to his will. Therefore, I announce in the name of Christ, that your sins are forgiven according to his promises in the Gospel. Amen.[16]

2. God shows his love for us in that while we were yet sinners Christ died for us.

God so loved the world that he gave his only Son, that whoever believes in him should not perish but have eternal life.

There is therefore now no condemnation for those who are in Christ Jesus. Amen.[16]

3. In A Responsive Form

Pastor: God so loved the world that he gave his only Son,

People: That whoever believes in him should not perish but have eternal life.

Pastor: Hear and say the gracious words of our Lord Jesus Christ for all who truly repent and turn to him:

People: Come to me, all who labor and are heavy laden, and I will give you rest.

Pastor: The grace of our Lord Jesus Christ be with you all.

People: Amen.[12]

COLLECT FOR CHRISTMAS

1. O God in the highest, by the birth of your beloved Son, you have made him to be for us both Word and Sacrament; grant that we may hear your word, receive your grace, and be made one with him who was born for our salvation, even Jesus Christ the Lord. Amen.[45]

2. O God, you have illumined this Holy Night with the light that is in Jesus Christ. May that light, whose mystery we have glimpsed in our present life, guide us also to the ultimate joy of eternal life, for the sake of Jesus Christ who lives and rules with you and the Holy Spirit now and ever. Amen.[46]

3. Lord Jesus, Child of Bethlehem, made human for the love of humankind, create in us a love so pure and perfect that all our desires are one with yours, in the unity of the Father and the Holy Spirit. Amen.[43]

ADVENT CANDLES, CHRISTMAS EVE (or CHRISTMAS DAY): GOOD NEWS[14]

INTRODUCTORY SENTENCES

Leader: Good evening (morning)! On this Christmas Eve (Day) we
are gathered as God's people to celebrate again what
Christ's coming means to the world. We join with Christians all over the world who are celebrating tonight
(today).

READING OF SCRIPTURE

A different person may read each passage: Isaiah 9:6; Luke
2:10, 14; Romans 5:5.

LIGHTING OF CANDLES

Leader: Tonight (Today) we relight the four Advent candles and
recall what the Good News means. (The leader lights a
candle as he/she says each word: hope, peace, love, joy.)
Jesus Christ is the greatest gift who makes other gifts possible. So, we light the Christ candle now, as we think what
Christ's coming means to each one of us.

PRAYER

Leader: We thank you, God, for your gift of Jesus Christ to the
whole world. We thank you that Christ's coming makes
hope, peace, love, and joy possible for every person in
every nation. Encourage us to do our part to bring good
will and peace to our families, our churches, our neigh-
borhoods, and the world. Now let your Spirit put us in
touch with you, the living God, through the words and
music we hear tonight (today). In the name of Jesus Christ
we pray. Amen.

HYMN

ECUMENICAL SCRIPTURE LESSONS FOR CYCLES A, B, AND C
Christmas Eve
A. Isaiah 62:1-4 You Shall be a Crown of Beauty
Colossians 1:15-20 Christ Will Be Honored
Luke 2:1-14 A Savior is Born
B. Isaiah 52:7-10 How Beautiful Upon the Mountains Are the
Feet
Hebrews 1:1-9 God Has Spoken to Us by His Son

John 1:1-14 The Word Was Made Flesh
C. Zechariah 2:10-13 Rejoice, O Daughter of Zion
Philippians 4:4-7 Rejoice In the Lord Always
Luke 2:15-20 The Shepherds said, "Let Us Go Over to Bethlehem"

Christmas Day
A. Isaiah 9:2, 6-7 Unto Us a Child is Born
Titus 2:11-15 God Gives Life to the World
Luke 2:1-14 A Savior is Born
Psalm 96 Tell of His Salvation
B. Isaiah 62:6-12 Raising Aloft the Banner of God
Colossians 1:15-20 He Has Made Known to Us the Mystery of His Will
Matthew 1:18-25 Emmanuel, God With Us
Psalm 98 He Has Done Marvelous Things
C. Isaiah 52:6-10 How Beautiful On the Mountains Are the Feet
Ephesians 1:3-10 In Him We Have Redemption
John 1:1-14 The Word Was Made Flesh
Psalm 97 Rejoice in the Lord, O You Righteous

PRAYERS AT THE ALTAR
Praise
Almighty God and Father of our Lord Jesus Christ: Praise be to you forever and ever. With angels and archangels and all the redeemed we glorify you, we praise you, we give thanks for all your wonders which you have given purely out of divine goodness and mercy without any merit or worthiness on our part. Especially do we thank you for your Gift to the world, our Lord Jesus Christ, who (AS ON THIS DAY) was made flesh, and dwelt among us, full of grace and truth.[37]

Enter into our hearts
Glory be to you, Lord Jesus Christ, our Savior for becoming poor that we might be made rich. We thank you for taking upon yourself our nature that we might become your followers and true children of the Father. O Lord Jesus Christ, true God and true man: Enter into our hearts and fill us with the grace of your tenderness and goodness. O you, who are the King of the high heavens: Establish your rule in our hearts and save us by your mercy from all misery of sin. Heal the wounds of misunderstanding, jealousy, or regret, and let the gentler air of the Christmas spirit touch our

lives, as though the cold of winter were touched by the kindlier breath of spring. Teach us to remember love, to forgive anger, to forget unkindness, that something of your beauty may be upon us, and that your grace may be in our hearts. Make us compassionate one toward another, merciful, tenderhearted, forgiving one another, even as you are compassionate toward us, forgiving our iniquities, transgressions, and sins.[51]

Intercessions

O Lord, our Savior, to whom glory is sung in the highest, while on earth peace is proclaimed to people of good will: Fill all the earth with your glory, and let your light shine upon all people who still sit in darkness and the shadow of death. Bring your redeemed from the east and west to the heritage of the saints, where with them and all the heavenly hosts we shall sing to the honor and glory of your holy name.[52]

Gather all Christian rulers about your manger and teach them to renew allegiance to you; and to use new scientific powers for the welfare of mankind. Encourage all Christians to serve as messengers of peace who recognize you as King. Grant that on this anniversary of your incarnation all parents and teachers may take to heart the message that children are sacred before you. Cause your praise to be chanted from their youthful lips. Since you have mercy on all who are poor, sick, or afflicted, refresh them with your comfort. Let the light and joy of this holy season enter their homes. Awaken and strengthen within them the living hope of their eternal salvation.[37]

SPECIAL INTERCESSIONS

Help all your children, almighty and eternal God, to celebrate the memory of Jesus' birth in the right spirit. Enable us to look to Jesus with true faith and joy; to love him as did Mary, to worship and honor him as do the holy angels. Give us grace to grow in his knowledge and cause us to serve him faithfully every day of the year.[6]

A prayer of St. Chrysostom

Almighty God, you have given us grace at this time, with one accord to make our common supplications to you, and your promise through your beloved Son that where two or three agree, you will grant their requests; fulfill now, O Lord, the desires and petitions of your servants, as may be most suitable for them;

granting us, in this world, knowledge of your truth, and in the world to come, life everlasting. Amen.[56]

WORDS OF WELCOME

1. We are happy to welcome all who are joining us in this joyful season as we worship God who sent his Son into the world, full of grace and truth. True to the Christian life, we know it and sing it sincerely:[12]

"How silently, how silently, the wondrous gift is given! So God imparts to human hearts the blessings of his heaven."
(Phillips Brooks)

2. We have come from a busy season preparing for Christmas. We are now together, happily coming to worship the newborn King. Let us rejoice and be glad. This is the day (night) the Lord has made us happy in adoration and prayer![12]

OFFERTORY SENTENCE

1. Each one must do as he has made up his mind, not reluctantly or under compulsion, for God loves a cheerful giver. (2 Corinthians 9:7)

2. For you know the grace of our Lord Jesus Christ, that though he was rich, yet for your sake he became poor, so that by his poverty you might become rich. (2 Corinthians 8:9)

OFFERTORY PRAYER

1. Gracious Lord, with every breath we thank you for life, energy, and hope. All that we have we receive from you each day. Accept, we pray, these offerings from the sweat of toil, the care of mind, and the love of thankful hearts, that we may serve Christ. Amen.[53]

2. O God, you blessed the whole world by the gift of your Son: Be pleased to accept our offering which we present to you with willing hearts. Bless it that others may know of your wonderful love, for the sake of him whose birth we celebrate. Amen.[12]

BLESSING OR BENEDICTION

1. The grace of the Lord Jesus Christ and the love of God and the fellowship of the Holy Spirit be with you all. Amen. (2 Corinthians 13:14)

2. A BLESSING

In the name of Christ who said, "I am with you always, to the close of the age," I want to offer this blessing: God be with you wherever you go! He will go before you to show you the way; To correct you when you take the wrong path; To encourage you when you lose heart; To share your joys and sorrows; To be your companion on life's way. In short, He stands and knocks at the door, To give you inner peace and strength. In the name of the Father, and of the Son and the Holy Spirit. Amen.[12]

6. THE FIRST SUNDAY AFTER CHRISTMAS

PRAYER FOR THE CHOIR
1. Eternal God, you gave your Son while glory was sung in the highest: Prepare our attitudes and control our spirits as we make ready to enter your courts, that the words we sing may spring from joyful hearts. Bless our congregation in this worship hour for Jesus' sake. Amen.[12]

2. Grant us, O Lord, the help of your Spirit in our hearts, that we may enter into your holy presence with reverence and gladness and render a service acceptable to you; through Jesus Christ our Lord. Amen.[57]

OPENING SENTENCES
1. A Responsive Form (Psalm 96:1-6)

Pastor: O sing to the Lord a new song; Sing to the Lord, all the earth!

People: Sing to the Lord, bless his name; tell of his salvation from day to day.

Pastor: Declare his glory among the nations, his marvelous works among all the peoples!

People: For great is the Lord, and greatly to be praised; He is to be feared above all gods.

Pastor: For all the gods of the peoples are idols; but the Lord made the heavens.

People: Honor and majesty are before him; Strength and beauty are in his sanctuary.

2. A Responsive Form (Psalm 96:7-9, 13)

Pastor: Ascribe to the Lord, O families of the peoples, ascribe to the Lord glory and strength!

People: Ascribe to the Lord the glory due his name; bring an offering, and come into his courts!

Pastor: Worship the Lord in holy array; tremble before him, all the earth!

People: For he comes to judge the earth.

All: He will judge the world with righteousness, and the peoples with his truth.

INVOCATION

1. Almighty God, you dwell in light unapproachable, whom no one has seen or can see; grant that we may know you in him whom you have given to be the light of the world, our Savior Jesus Christ, and in the joy of his Gospel may worship you in spirit and in truth. Amen.[22]

2. O Lord our God, you have bidden the light to shine out of darkness and have again wakened us to praise your goodness and ask for your grace; accept now, in your endless mercy, the sacrifice of our worship and thanksgiving, and grant to us all such requests as may be wholesome for us. Make us to be children of the light and of the day, and heirs of your everlasting inheritance. Remember, O Lord, according to the multitude of your mercies, your whole Church; all who join with us in prayer; and all brothers and sisters by land or sea, or wherever they may be in your vast kingdom, who stand in need of your grace and guidance. Pour out upon them the riches of your mercy, so that we, redeemed in soul and body, and steadfast in faith, may ever praise your wonderful and holy name; through Jesus Christ our Lord. Amen.[54]

CALL TO CONFESSION OF SINS

1. Hear the promises of God: "Ask, and it will be given you; seek and you will find; knock, and it will be opened to you." "If we confess our sins, he is faithful and just, and will forgive our sins."[16]

2. Let us humbly confess our sins to God, beseeching him, in the name of our Lord Jesus Christ, to grant us forgiveness.[58]

CONFESSION OF SINS

1. We confess to you, almighty God, that we have sinned in thought, word, and deed. Make us truly contrite. Forgive us! And give us grace to amend our lives according to your Word, for the glory of your holy name. Through Jesus Christ our Lord. Amen.[55]

2. Almighty God, our maker and redeemer: We poor sinners confess to you that we are by nature sinful and unclean, and that we have sinned against you by thought, word, and deed. Wherefore we flee for refuge to your infinite mercy, seeking and imploring your grace, for the sake of our Lord Jesus Christ. Amen.[58]

ASSURANCE OF PARDON

1. Upon this humble confession which you have made, as a minister of the Lord Jesus Christ, and by his authority, I declare to you, who do truly repent and heartily believe in Jesus Christ, and are sincerely determined to amend your sinful life, the forgiveness of all your sins in the name of the Father and of the Son and of the Holy Spirit. Amen.[6]

2. Hearken now to the comforting assurance of the grace of God, promised in the Gospel to all who repent and believe: As I live, says the Lord God, I have no pleasure in the death of the wicked, but that the wicked turn from his way and live. God so loved the world that he gave his only Son, that whoever believes in him should not perish, but have eternal life.

To as many of you, therefore, who truly repent of your sins, and believe in the Lord Jesus with full purpose of new obedience, I announce and declare, by the authority and in the name of Christ, that your sins are forgiven, according to his promise in the Gospel; through Jesus Christ our Lord. Amen.[3]

COLLECT

1. Lord God, who formed the earth for our habitation, make your Word so evident in our midst, that all false gods shall be left behind, and that every knee shall bow to you and every tongue declare the triumph of your strength and glory; through Christ our Savior. Amen.[60]

2. O Lord, heavenly Father, who through your angels visited poor shepherds of the field to calm their fear and rejoice that Christ the Savior was born; drive away, we beseech you, all fear from our hearts, and stir up in us this true and rightful joy, that, though here on earth we may be despised, miserable, poor, and forlorn, we may nevertheless be comforted and rejoice that we have your dear Son, Christ our Lord, as our Savior, who for our sake became human, that he might defend us from death and evil and save us forever. Amen.[59]

ECUMENICAL SCRIPTURE LESSONS FOR CYCLES A, B, AND C

A. Ecclesiastes 3:1-9, 14-17 For Everything There is a Season
Colossians 3:12-17 That Christ May Dwell in Your Hearts Through Faith
Matthew 2:13-15, 19-23 The Flight into Egypt

Psalm 111 He Sent Redemption to His People
B. Jeremiah 31:10-13 I Will Comfort Them
Hebrews 2:10-18 Made Like His Brothers
Luke 2:25-35 Adoration and Prophecy of Simeon
Psalm 111 He Sent Redemption to His People
C. Isaiah 45:18-22 Turn to Me and Be Saved
Romans 11:33—12:2 O The Depth of the Riches and Wisdom and Knowledge of God!
Luke 2:41-52 The Boy Jesus in the Temple
Psalm 111 He Sent Redemption to His People

PRAYERS AT THE ALTAR
Praise
Almighty God, Creator and Ruler of all worlds, in the beginning you commanded the light to shine out of darkness: We bless you that when the fullness of time came, you gave the light of the knowledge of your glory in the face of Jesus Christ. We bless you, we worship you, we glorify you, we give thanks for your great glory, O God, Heavenly King, God the Father Almighty, that by the incarnation of your Son you have fulfilled the promise of the ages and revealed your love to people. We adore you for the love which brought the Lord of glory down to the manger of humiliation. We praise you that he dwelt among us, full of grace and truth. We thank you for the light that dawned through him upon our darkness, for the saving hope which he kindled, and the redemption he purchased. We bless you that in him we know you as our Father, and one another as your children, called to love and forgive and serve as he gave example. Praise be to you, O Lord God, for you have visited and redeemed your people.[31]

At the close of the old year
O Lord, you have been our dwelling place in all generations; you existed before the mountains were brought forth, or ever you formed the earth and the world, even from everlasting to everlasting: We thank you for all the blessings which you have granted to us during the *past year*. We remember the days of the year now almost gone and humbly bow in gratitude to you for bearing with us in patience and long-suffering.[6]

Help us to follow
O Lord Jesus Christ, the Beginning and the End, the First and the Last: We would end the old and begin the new year with you.

Enable us henceforth to abide in you, and let your words abide in us, that we may glorify you in good works and holy lives. Help us to lay to heart the wisdom you have been teaching us, and, forgetting the things that would come between us and you, to look to you for guidance, and follow you all our days.[31]

Triumph over our infirmities

For the *new year* which we are about to enter, cause your grace to triumph over our infirmities, and grant us inwardly such increased steadfastness, that through sunshine and storm, we may trust and not be afraid, work and not be weary, suffer and not complain. Help us to overcome all evil with patience, and to possess our souls in humility.[22]

For the universal church

Gracious Father: We humbly beseech you for the universal Church. Fill it with all truth, and in all truth with peace. Where it is corrupt, purify it; where it is in error, correct it; where anything is amiss, reform it; where it is right, strengthen and confirm it; where it is in want, furnish it; and where it is divided and rent asunder, heal it.[42]

For the coming of God's Kingdom and peace

O you King eternal, immortal, invisible, you only wise God, our Savior: Hasten the coming of your Kingdom upon earth, and draw the whole of humankind into willing obedience to your rule. Overcome all enemies of Christ and bring low every power that is exalted against him. Cast out all the evil things which cause fightings among us and let your Spirit rule the hearts of men in righteousness and love.[10]

WELCOME TO VISITORS

1. We are glad you are with us during this Christmas season. We have been glad to see college students and others in family reunions among us and we wish them well as they resume their activities. Worship with us again![12]

2. To all who are *young* and need counsel; to all who are *strong* and want a task; to all who are *weary* and need rest; to all who are *lonely* and want companionship; to all who *mourn* and need comforting; to all who are *burdened* with sin and need a Savior; to *EVERYONE,* this church opens wide its doors and in the name of Christ our Lord says, "Welcome!"[4]

OFFERTORY SENTENCE

1. And the King will answer them, "Truly, I say to you, as you did it to one of the least of these my brethren, you did it to me." (Matthew 25:40)

2. The point is this: he who sows sparingly will also reap sparingly, and he who sows bountifully will also reap bountifully. (2 Corinthians 9:6)

OFFERTORY PRAYER

1. O giver of every good and perfect gift: We acknowledge your bounty in these gifts which we now offer and dedicate to you. We pray that you will accept them and multiply them for the work of your Church. Through Jesus Christ our Lord. Amen.[66]

2. All-gracious God, who of your infinite love gave your Son Jesus Christ to be born in Bethlehem, to die near Jerusalem, and rise again for our justification, and have made us partakers of the divine nature through the gift of the Holy Spirit: Accept the offering which we now present to you; and grant that our bodies, souls, and spirits may be to you a living sacrifice, holy and well pleasing in your sight; and that going forth in your strength, we may be able truly to serve you, and in all things to obey your will. Through Jesus Christ our Lord. Amen.[10]

BLESSING OR BENEDICTION

1. The peace of God, which passes all understanding, keep your hearts and minds in the knowledge and love of God, and of his Son Jesus Christ our Lord; and the blessing of God Almighty, the Father, the Son, and the Holy Spirit, be upon you, and remain with you always. Amen.[49]

2. The Lord bless you, and keep you: The Lord make his face shine upon you, and be gracious unto you: The Lord lift up his countenance upon you, and give you peace. (Numbers 6:24-26)

7. SECOND SUNDAY AFTER CHRISTMAS

PRAYER FOR THE CHOIR

1. Open our lips, O Lord, and our mouths shall show forth your praise. Inspire these choir members who have consecrated to your service the gift of song. So sustain them in their guidance of the congregation now met to praise you, that your holy name may be glorified, and your people truly rejoice in your presence. Help them as they worship in your sanctuary and lead the songs of Zion, that they shall be acceptable to you in this their office, and make all your people joyful; through Jesus Christ our Lord. Amen.[36]

2. How lovely is your dwelling place, O Lord of hosts! Accept the longing of our souls for your courts, O Lord, and bless us as we lead others in worship that all may worship in spirit and in truth. Through Jesus Christ our Lord. Amen.[12]

OPENING SENTENCES OR CALL TO WORSHIP

Any of the following sentences may be said:

1. The Lord is in his holy temple; let all the earth keep silence before him. (Habakkuk 2:20)

2. O come, let us worship and bow down, let us kneel before the Lord, our Maker! For he is our God, and we are the people of his pasture, and the sheep of his hand. (Psalm 95:6-7)

3. God is spirit, and those who worship him must worship in spirit and truth. (John 4:24)

4. Our help is in the name of the Lord, who made heaven and earth. (Psalm 124:8)

5. Make a joyful noise to the Lord, all the lands! Serve the Lord with gladness! (Psalm 100:1-2a)

INVOCATION

1. O God, you appoint all things to a destined and holy end, and you require of us a reasonable service; quicken in us the sense of a gracious presence and power in the world, of a providence that never slumbers, of a love that never fails, and so unite us with yourself in our aspirations and thoughts that, with our whole might doing those things which please you, we may live in your favor and in that light which ever broadens to the perfect day. Keep us

this day, we beseech you, without fear, without sin, without distrust, and, through meditation and prayer, prepare us for another week of faithful labor and generous service; through Jesus Christ our Lord. Amen.[22]

2. O Lord, our God. You are the life of all, the help of those who flee to you, and the hope of those who cry to you: Look mercifully upon us! Cleanse our minds and hearts that with a clear conscience and a calm hope we may confidently worship you. Through Jesus Christ our Lord. Amen.[2]

CALL TO CONFESSION

1. Beloved in the Lord, if we say we have no sin, we deceive ourselves, and the truth is not in us. If we confess our sins, God is faithful and just, and will forgive our sins and will cleanse us from all unrighteousness. Let us, therefore, humble ourselves before the throne of almighty God, our heavenly Father, and confess our manifold sins and transgressions with lowly and contrite hearts, that we may obtain forgiveness of the same through the merits of our Lord Jesus Christ.[56]

2. Knowing that God has shown us the way, the truth, and the life in Jesus Christ, we are humbly aware of our sins and shortcomings. But in him we dare to come with confidence, asking him to forgive us, saying:[12]

CONFESSION OF SINS

1. Lord of all might and compassion, you know and remember our weaknesses; we humbly confess the evil we have done and our weariness in well-doing, the vows we have broken, the duties we have refused, the hours we have lightly spent without any gracious deed, the tasks undone which proclaim us idle and unprofitable servants, and all our many transgressions, shortcomings, and offenses. Have compassion on our unworthiness, we beseech you; create in us a sincere desire for whatever things are true, just, honorable, pure, and of good report; mold us inwardly to your will; and in the end we will be more than conquerors through him who loved us and gave himself for us. Amen.[22]

2. God of mercy and healing, help us to confess our sin against you and against our neighbors. We choose the easy wrong rather than the hard right; we prefer to walk in darkness rather than light; we would rather enjoy our sins than bare them before you. Search

us, O God, and know us. Create in us clean hearts; for between our sins and their rewards we would set the sacrifice of Christ our Lord. Amen.[62]

ASSURANCE OF PARDON

1. Who is in a position to condemn? Only Christ. And Christ died for us, Christ rose for us, Christ reigns in power for us, Christ prays for us.

If a man is in Christ, he becomes a new creature altogether — the past is finished and gone, everything has become fresh and new.

Friends: Believe the good news of the Gospel. *In Jesus Christ we are forgiven.*

Let us now obey the Lord. This is his command: to give allegiance to his Son, Jesus Christ and to love one another.

Give thanks to God, for he is good, his love is everlasting. *You are the Lord, giver of mercy! You are the Christ, giver of mercy! You are the Lord, giver of mercy!*[67]

2. Hear the Good News! This statement is completely reliable and should be universally accepted: Christ Jesus entered the world to rescue sinners. He personally bore our sins in his body on the cross, so that we might be dead to sin and be alive to all that is good. Friends: Believe the good news of the Gospel. In Jesus Christ, we are forgiven.

As God's own people, be merciful in action, kindly in heart, humble in mind. Be always ready to forgive as freely as the Lord has forgiven you. And, above everything else, be loving, and never forget to be thankful for what God has done for you.[67]

COLLECT

1. O God, in the birth of your Holy Child, Jesus, you have visited and redeemed your people. Grant that he may be born in us so that we may share his joy and peace, and be strengthened to worship and serve you acceptably through him, our Lord and Savior Jesus Christ. Amen.[63]

2. God our Father, we thank you that you have caused your light to shine in darkness, your glory to be revealed where it is least expected, and that this continues to be your way. We give you thanks for the fullness of your grace in Jesus our Savior. We thank you for the humble shepherds and the loving Mother, and

for all that light breaking through our darkness. Glory be to you,
O God most high. Amen.[22]

ECUMENICAL SCRIPTURE LESSONS FOR CYCLES A, B, AND C

A. Proverbs 8:22-31 The Lord Created Me at the Beginning of
   His Work
   Ephesians 1:15-23 He Has Put All Things Under His Feet
   John 1:1-5, 9-14 The Revelation of the Word Made Flesh
   Psalm 147:12-20 Praise Your God, O Zion
B. Isaiah 60:1-5 Arise, Shine; For Your Light Has Come
   Revelation 21:22-22:2 And I Saw My Temple in the City
   Luke 2:21-24 Now Lettest Thou Thy Servant Depart In Peace
   Psalm 147:12-20 Praise Your God, O Zion
C. Job 28:20-28 The Fear of the Lord, That is Wisdom
   1 Corinthians 1:18-25 For the Foolishness of God is Wiser
   Than Men
   Luke 2:36-40 Anna Spoke of Him to All
   Psalm 147:12-20 Praise Your God, O Zion

PRAYERS AT THE ALTAR
Thanks for the past year
O God, our merciful Father in Christ Jesus our Lord: at the beginning of this year of our pilgrimage we come before you with
thanksgiving. We praise your glorious name for the countless and
unmerited mercies which you have bestowed upon us during our
whole life and especially during the year that has just closed.[6]
Help us in the new year
O you who are from everlasting to everlasting, without beginning or end of days: Replenish us with heavenly grace, at the beginning of this year, that we may be enabled to accept all its duties,
to perform all its labors, to welcome all its mercies, to meet all
its trials, and to advance through all it holds in store for us, with
cheerful courage and a constant mind.[10]
A general thanksgiving
Almighty God, Father of all mercies, we, your unworthy servants, do give you most humble and hearty thanks for all your
goodness and loving-kindness to us, and to all people. We praise
you for our creation, preservation, and all the blessings of this life;
but above all, for your boundless love in the redemption of the
world by our Lord Jesus Christ, for the means of grace, and for

the hope of glory. And, we beseech you, give us that due sense of all your mercies, that our hearts may be sincerely thankful, and that we may show forth your praise, not only with our lips, but also in our lives, by giving up ourselves to your service, and by walking before you in holiness and righteousness all our days; through Jesus Christ, our Lord, to whom, with you and the Holy Spirit be all honor and glory, world without end. Amen.[56]

A prayer for spiritual victory

God of all power and glory, who has not appointed us unto wrath, but to obtain salvation by our Lord Jesus Christ, perfect and fulfill in us, we beseech you, the work of your redeeming mercy, that, being delivered more and more from our sins, we may be able to serve you in newness of life. Sanctify us wholly, that we may overcome the world. Give us courage to confess Christ always and to give ourselves joyfully in his service, that we may rest in hope and attain finally to the resurrection of the just; through the infinite merits of our Savior, Jesus Christ. Amen.[56]

A prayer for the church universal

O God and Father of our Lord Jesus Christ, of whom the whole family in heaven and earth is named, cause your blessing, we beseech you, to rest upon the Church, which he has redeemed with his most precious blood. Enlighten her ministers by your Word; support her congregations with your grace. Deliver her from false doctrine, heresy and schism. Enable her to keep the unity of the spirit in the bond of peace, and clothe her with the beauty of holiness. Establish and reveal your glory among all nations. By the working of your Providence destroy all wicked devices against your holy Word, and bring in speedily the full victory of your everlasting kingdom; through Jesus Christ our Lord. Amen.[56]

A prayer for the President or Prime Minister and all others in authority

Almighty God, whose kingdom is from everlasting to everlasting, look with favor upon your servants, the (President, Prime Minister), the governor of this (state, commonwealth), and all others in authority. So rule their hearts and bless their endeavors that law and order, justice and peace, may everywhere prevail. Preserve us from national sins and corruption. Make us strong and great in the fear of the Lord and in the love of righteousness, reverent in the use of freedom, just in the exercise of power, generous in the protection of the helpless, so that we may become a blessing to all nations, through Jesus Christ our Lord. Amen.[56]

A prayer for all conditions of men

O God, the Creator and Preserver of all humankind, we implore your mercy in behalf of all classes and conditions of people, that it may please you to visit them with your most compassionate help, according to their manifold necessities and wants. Especially do we beseech you to have pity upon all widows and orphans, upon all prisoners and captives, upon all sick and dying persons, upon all such as are persecuted for righteousness' sake. Enable them to look unto you, O most merciful Father, and to call upon your name, that they may find you a present Savior in their affliction and distress. May it please you to deliver them, and raise them up in due time, giving them patience under all their suffering, the rich comfort of your grace here below, and eternal rest with you in heaven; through our Lord Jesus Christ. Amen.[56]

(HERE MAY BE OFFERED A MEMORIAL PRAYER OR OTHER SPECIAL PRAYERS)

A prayer of St. Chrysostom

Almighty God, you have given us grace at this time with one accord to make our common supplications to you, and your promise that where two or three are gathered together in your name, you will grant their requests, fulfill now, O Lord, the desires and petitions of your servants, as may be most expedient for them, granting us, in this world, knowledge of your truth, and, in the world to come, life everlasting. Amen.[56]

WELCOME TO VISITORS

1. To all who desire to learn of him who is the way, the truth, and the life, this church bids a cordial welcome. May every visitor find this to be a house of prayer where we are all guests of God and Christian workers.[12]

2. We extend a hearty welcome and sincere greeting to all who are with us. On behalf of all our members we especially greet our visitors. We hope you will find inspiration and strength for whatever daily tasks and duties you face during the week.[12]

OFFERTORY SENTENCE

In recognition of God's Lordship over all, David said, "For all things come from thee, and of thy own have we given thee." (1 Chronicles 29:14b)

2. Each one must do as he has made up his mind, not reluctantly or under compulsion, for God loves a cheerful giver. (2 Corinthians 9:7)

OFFERTORY PRAYER

1. O Lord our God, King of all the earth, you have given us all things richly to enjoy: Accept now of your infinite goodness the offerings of your people, which in obedience to your commandment, and in honor of your name they yield and dedicate to you; and grant to us your blessing, that the same being devoted to your service may be used for your glory; through Jesus Christ our Lord. Amen.[17]

2. Gracious Lord, with every breath we give you thanks for life, energy, and hope. All that we have we receive from you each day. Accept, we pray, these offerings from the sweat of toil, the care of mind, and the love of thankful hearts, that we may serve Christ. Amen.[53]

BLESSING OR BENEDICTION

1. The God of peace who brought again from the dead our Lord Jesus, the great shepherd of the sheep, by the blood of the eternal covenant, equip you with everything good that you may do his will, working in you that which is pleasing in his sight, through Jesus Christ; to whom be glory for ever and ever. Amen. (Hebrews 13:20)

2. Now may our Lord Jesus Christ himself, and God our Father, who loved us and gave us eternal comfort and good hope through grace, comfort your hearts and establish them in every good work and word. Amen. (2 Thessalonians 2:16-17)

C. A Brief Treasury
of Additional Worship Resources

ASSURANCE OF PARDON

1. Almighty God, who freely pardons all who repent and turn to him, now fulfill in every contrite heart the promise of redeeming grace, remitting all our sins, and cleansing us from an evil conscience, through the perfect sacrifice of Christ Jesus our Lord. Amen.[61]

2. God so loved the world, that he gave his only Son, that whoever believes in him should not perish, but have eternal life.

Hear the gracious words of our Lord Jesus Christ to all who repent and turn to him:

Come to me, all who labor and are heavy laden, and I will give you rest.

Him that comes to me I will in no wise cast out.

The grace of the Lord Jesus Christ be with you all. Amen.[10]

FOR THE NEWLY MARRIED

1. We recall loved ones who have recently exchanged rings in holy wedlock. The names of _____ and _____ come to mind. Bless them in their life together as they seek guidance and strength in their relationships and responsibilities.[12]

2. O God of love, you did wonderfully bless the mother and home of our Lord Jesus, bless the new home formed by the marriage of _____ and _____. Guide them in faithfulness, consideration, and their growing commitment.[12]

FOR THOSE WHO MOURN

1. We remember before you all whose hearts are troubled by the separation of death. Comfort them and grant them peace for their anxiety. We pray for the families and friends of _____ whom we name before you.[12]

2. Eternal God, you abide, though your children pass away, and are ever near to uphold and bless. Remember in your mercy the family of _____ whom we mention by name. Give strength and guidance to them as they return to the duties of life with renewed seriousness and purpose.[12]

FOR JOY IN GOD'S CREATION

O heavenly Father, you have filled the world with beauty. Open our eyes to behold your gracious hand in all your works that, rejoicing in your whole creation, we may learn to serve you with gladness; for the sake of him through whom all things were made, your Son Jesus Christ our Lord. Amen.[8]

FOR PEACE

Eternal God, in your perfect kingdom no sword is drawn but the sword of righteousness, no strength known but the strength of love. So mightily spread abroad your Spirit, that all people may be gathered under the banner of the Prince of Peace, as children of one Father; to whom be dominion and glory, now and for ever. Amen.[8]

FOR THE HUMAN FAMILY

O God, you made us in your own image and redeemed us through Jesus your Son: Look with compassion on the whole human family; take away the arrogance and hatred which infect our hearts; break down the walls that separate us; unite us in bonds of love; and work through our struggle and confusion to accomplish your purposes on earth that, in your good time, all nations and races may serve you in harmony around your heavenly throne; through Jesus Christ our Lord. Amen.[8]

FOR THE PARISH OR THE CONGREGATION

Almighty and everliving God, ruler of all things in heaven and earth, hear our prayers for this parish family. Strengthen the faithful, arouse the careless, and restore the penitent. Grant us all things necessary for our common life, and bring us all to be of one heart and mind within your holy Church; through Jesus Christ our Lord. Amen.[8]

FOR THE GOOD USE OF LEISURE

O God, in the course of this busy life, give us times of refreshment and peace; and grant that we may so use our leisure to rebuild our bodies and renew our minds, that our spirits may be opened to the goodness of your creation; through Jesus Christ our Lord. Amen.[8]

FOR TRAVELERS

O God, our heavenly Father, whose glory fills the whole creation, and whose presence we find wherever we go; preserve those who travel (in particular _____); surround *them* with your loving care; protect them from every danger; and bring them in safety to their journey's end; through Jesus Christ our Lord. Amen [8]

FOR THE SICK

Almighty Father, giver of life and health; look mercifully, we beseech you, on the sick and suffering, especially those for whom our prayers are desired, that by your blessing upon them and upon those who minister to them, they may be restored, if it be your gracious will, to health of body and mind, and give thanks to you in your holy Church; through Jesus Christ our Lord. Amen.[3]

FOR THOSE IN DISTRESS

O God, you see all the suffering, injustice, and misery in this world; have pity, we implore you, on the work of your hands. Look mercifully upon the poor, the oppressed, and all who are heavy-laden with error, labor, or sorrow. Fill our hearts with deep compassion for all who suffer, and hasten the coming of your kingdom of justice and truth; for the sake of Jesus Christ our Lord. Amen.[3]

FOR SERVICE MEN AND WOMEN

O God of grace, we pray for the young men and women from our midst now in the armed forces of our country. Enable them to keep their visions fresh and their ideals high in these difficult times.[12]

Grant to the leaders of our national life knowledge of your ways, good judgment between things more and things less important, that they may guide wisely whatever portion of destiny may be in their keeping. Guide those who are guiding us![12]

We ask for your comforting help for those from whom the young men and women in the service have been separated. Grant that, drawing nearer to you, they who are gone and we who are here may be bound together by your love in the communion of your Holy Spirit, and in the fellowship of Christians everywhere.[12]

FOR LEADERS OF THE PEOPLE

O Lord, our heavenly Father, the high and mighty Ruler of the universe, you behold all dwellers upon earth; most heartily we beseech you with your favor to behold and bless your servant, the President of these United States, and all who make or execute our laws; and so replenish them with the graces of your Holy Spirit that they may always incline to your will, and walk in your way. Endow them plenteously with heavenly gifts; grant them health and prosperity with a strong sense of justice and fairness to all.[7]

COMMISSIONS

1. Go forth into the world in peace; be of good courage; hold fast to that which is good; render to no one evil for evil; strengthen the fainthearted; support the weak; help the afflicted; honor all people; love and serve the Lord, rejoicing in the power of the Holy Spirit.[16]

2. Go forth to be good servants and friends of him who comes preaching good tidings, binding up the broken hearted, proclaiming liberty to the captives, and comforting all who mourn. May he guide your feet finally in paths of helpfulness.[12]

3. You have come to worship, to give, to pray, to learn, and to sing. Now go to serve, to share, to give, to witness, and to love. And do it joyfully in the presence of our Savior, Jesus Christ.[33]

A CLOSING PRAYER OR CHALLENGE
If any true word

If any true word of yours has been spoken to us, if any ray of your heavenly light has shone upon us, if any righteous purpose has arisen within us, may we be found faithful to what we have received, that all our thoughts and actions may henceforth be more in harmony with your will. Let your blessing be upon our going out and our coming in now and evermore. Amen.[28]

D. Sources

The author of this book finds himself deeply indebted to many people. A number after the prayers in the body of the book refers to the sources listed below. In some cases material as it appears in the present volume has been adapted.

1. Morgan, J. Richmond. *Church Management,* (December, 1938.)

2. *Coptic Liturgy of St. Basil,* fourth century.

3. *Book of Worship.* General Synod of the Evangelical and Reformed Church. (Cleveland: Central Publishing House, 1947).

4. Adapted by the author from an unknown source.

5. *The Book of Common Order* of the Presbyterian Church of Canada, 1948.

6. *Evangelical Book of Worship.* Published by the German Evangelical Synod of North America. (St. Louis and Chicago: Eden Publishing House, 1916).

7. *The Book of Common Prayer.* According to the Use of the Protestant Episcopal Church in the U.S.A. Revised Edition. Oxford University Press, 1932.

8. *The Book of Common Prayer* and Administration of the Sacraments and Other Rites and Ceremonies of the Church Together with The Psalter or Psalms of David According to the Use of The Episcopal Church, the Church Hymnal Corporation, New York and the Seabury Press, 1977, copyright by Charles Mortimer Guilbert.

9. *The Kingdom, the Power and the Glory.* Services of Praise and Prayer for Occasional Use in Churches. An American edition of *The Grey Book.* (New York: Oxford University Press, 1933).

10. *The Book of Common Worship.* The Presbyterian Board of Publication and Sabbath-School Work, Philadelphia, 1906.

11. Newton, Joseph Fort, quoted in Palmer's *Aids to Worship.*

12. Rest, Friedrich.

13. *Evangelical Book of Worship.* Prayer (see Source #6) combined with *The Book of Worship for Church and Home,* The Methodist Publishing House, 1944, 1945.

14. *Advent: A Congregational Life/Intergenerational Experience,* United Church Press, Copyright 1977, as presented in Source #21.

15. *Gelasian Sacramentary.* A.D. 494.

16. *Services of the Church,* Service of Word and Sacrament I, II, An Order For Morning Worship. (Philadelphia: United Church Press, 1966 and 1969).

17. *Service Book and Ordinal of the Presbyterian Church of South Africa.* Second Edition (Glasgow: Jackson, Son and Company, 1929).

18. Bright, William, *Ancient Collects.* James Parker and Company, Oxford and Longdon. Compiled in 1875.

19. *Services of the Church,* the Collects for the Christian Year. (Philadelphia: United Church Press, 1969).

20. Johnstone, Margaret Blaine.

21. *Proposed Services of the Congregation's Life, Test Document,* Office for Church Life and Leadership, United Church of Christ, 1982.

22. Cameron, Hugh, *Prayers for Use In Public Worship.* (Edinburgh: Alexander Brunton, 1921).

23. Noyes, Morgan Phelps, *Prayers for Services.* (New York, London: Charles Scribner's Sons, 1935).

24. Combined from Source #6 and Source #40.

25. Gordon, Ernst, in Source #29.

26. Glover, Carl A., *The Lectern: A Book of Public Prayers.* (New York, Nashville: Abingdon-Cokesbury Press, 1946).

27. Aquinas, Thomas.

28. Kennedy, J. Linwood, from one of his church bulletins. He in turn is indebted to Faith Presbyterian Church, Fairfax, Virginia.

29. Davies, Horton, in *Prayers & Other Resources for Public Worship,* by Horton Davies and Morris Slifer, 1976. Copyright by Abingdon.

30. Annemanth, van Lelyfeld. From worship materials received by the Commission on Worship, UCC.

31. *Prayers for the Christian Year.* Prepared by a Committee of the Church of Scotland. Oxford University Press, Glasgow, Edinburgh, London, New York, etc. 1935.

32. Davies, Horton M. From a manuscript of the Commission on Worship, UCC.

33. Koopman, LeRoy, *Book of Worship Aids.* (Palm Springs, Florida: Sunday Publications, 1976.)

34. Davies, Horton M., in *Services of the Church, The Collects for the Christian Year,* United Church Press, Copyright 1969.

35. Beebe, David. From worship materials in The Commission on Worship, UCC.

36. Simpson, Hubert L., *Let Us Worship God.* (London: James Clarke and Company, 1928).

37. Source # and *Church Book for the Use of Evangelical Lutheran Congregations.* (Philadelphia: J. K Shryock, 1893).

38. *The Book of Common Order,* published by Oxford University Press, and used by permission of the Committee on Public Worship and Aids to Devotion of the Church of Scotland.

39. Newbigin, Leslie, from a manuscript on worship of the Commission on Worship, UCC.

40. *The Book of Common Worship (Revised Edition).* The Board of Christian Education of The Presbyterian Church, U.S.A., Philadelphia, 1932.

41. Suter, John Wallace, *Prayers of the Spirit.* (New York, London: Harper and Brothers, 1943).

42. Laude, Archbishop William.

43. From *The Book of Common Worship.* Provisional Services. (The Westminster Press, 1966). Used by permission.

44. Jentsch, T. W., from a worship manuscript in the Commission on Worship, UCC.

45. Selby, Donald J., as in Source #29.

46. Jentsche, T. W., in worship material compiled by the Commission on Worship, UCC.

47. Adapted from *Armenian Liturgy.*

48. Augustine, St.

49. *Book of Common Worship.* For use in the several Communions of the Church of Christ. Wilbur Thirkfield and Oliver Huckel, editors. (E. P. Dutton and Company, Inc., 1932).

50. Jones, R. C., *A Book of Prayers.* William and Norgate, London, 19th Century.

51. Peabody, Francis Greenwood, *Prayers for Various Occasions and Needs.* (Boston, New York: Houghton Mifflin Company, 1930).

52. Mozarabic Liturgy. Before A.D. 700. Combined with #.

53. Kirkland, Bryant.

54. Greek Church Liturgy, Third Century.

55. Bloesch, Paul.

56. *The Order of Worship for the Lord's Day.* A service for provisional use, Committee on Liturgies, Evangelical and Reformed Church, 1958.

57. *A Book of Offices and Prayers for Priest and People.* Compiled by two Presbyters of the Church. (New York: Edwin S. Gorham, Inc., 1927).

58. *Common Service Book of the Lutheran Church.* The General

Synod of the Evangelical Lutheran Church in the U.S.A., 1917.

59. Veit, Dietrich, *Kinderpostille,* 1549, in J. W. Doberstein's *Minister's Prayer Book,* Muhlenberg, 1959.

60. Paine, R. Howard. In Source #19.

61. *The Book of Common Worship.* The Board of Christian Education of the Presbyterian Church in the U.S.A., Philadelphia, Revised, 1946.

62. Brenner, Scott, in Source #29.

63. Slifer, Morris D., in Source #19.

64. *The Book of Worship for Church and Home.* The Methodist Publishing House, 1944, 1945.

65. Newman, Cardinal John in Source #7.

66. Morrison, James Dalton. *Minister's Service Book,* for Pulpit and Parish Use. (Chicago and New York: Willett Clark and Company, 1937).

67. *The Worshipbook — Services and Hymns,* MCMLXX, MCMLXII, Copyright, Westminster Press, Philadelphia.